Being a Photographer

By Laurie Young

First Published 2014
by Frozen Event Ltd.

© 2014 Laurie Young All rights reserved.
ISBN 978-1-234-56789-1

The right of Laurie Young to be identified as author of this work has been asserted in accordance with sections 77 and 78 of the Copyright, Designs and Patents Act 1988.

Notices
Product or corporate names may be trademarks or registered trademarks, and are used only for identification en explanation with intent to infringe.

Dedication

This book is dedicated to the spirit of always learning

About the cover photo

The front cover photo is the only photo I use in this book. As such, it's the only chance I get to demonstrate by example what I mean when I talk about the intent of a photo.

A book cover is important. It needs to attract attention, and it needs to set the tone for the book. A reader forms their first impression of a book's content based on the cover. If they then find that the actual content is something quite different then they are, at best, going to feel the cover is bad, and at worse feel betrayed.

In choosing a cover design for this book I had a very clear intent in mind:

o I had to use a photo (it is a book on photography after all!)
o I wanted to make the point that a photo doesn't have to be technically perfect to be effective. The photo I've used is intentionally blurry, too dark, and by many criteria, a bad photo.

- I wanted the photo to be interesting enough to engage the viewer's attention.
- I wanted to set the tone of thinking about what photo to take. To me, that question is conjured up every time I pack my camera bag and try to work out what equipment to take, it depends on what photo I plan on taking!

So when you look at the cover photo, and form your own opinion of whether or not it's a good photo, remember that it was chosen to do a particular job. The question of whether or not it is a good photo only makes sense when that job is kept in mind.

About the Author

Laurie lives and works in London. He holds a masters degree in physics and a doctorate in computer science, both from Imperial College London, where he also ran the photographic society. As a physics student he found the technical questions of shutter speeds, ISO and aperture reasonably straight forward, but found something new and challenging in the question of what to take photos of and why.

Today he is passionate about technology entrepreneurship, photography and dance. He spends his time learning and passing on what he has learned.

His online home is www.wildfalcon.com and he can be found on Twitter as @LRY_Photo

Forword

Over the past decade or so, I've written a modest number of books about photography. In the process, I've explained how aperture works, what ISO is, and how to make sense of hyper-focal distances more often than I care to remember.

Perhaps surprisingly, one thing I've not spent a lot of time thinking about, is why people get so passionate about photography. What is it about a photograph that seems to set people's imaginations a-flutter? Is it just a desire to document the world around us? Perhaps a drive to find the most visually appealing representation of the world around us?

Taking that same line of questioning even deeper - what does it mean to be a photographer? Is it simply an artistic application of the oft-clinical science of Physics, or is there something more to it?

Grab a pen, and jot down some notes: Who are you taking photos for, how does your audience affect your photographic output, and how much are you willing to push the creative, technical, and philosophical boundaries of the work you produce, depending on who will consume your images?

Laurie Young tackles all of these questions in an incredibly refreshing way, starting with asking a question so basic that most people don't even pause to give it some thought. Which is a terrible shame, because it's a crucial part of developing as a photographer - both as an artist, and as a technician.

As a writer, the first thing you do is to define your audience - only by knowing who you are speaking to, can you hope to reach them in a meaningful way. That so few people go through the same thought process as a photographer is a terrible waste. I'm not exaggerating that this book has completely changed how I view photography - both my own, and that of others.

And for that reason alone, it's worth reading this book twice: Once to grok the concept, and once to completely readjust your perspective on your own photography.

Haje Jan Kamps
London, 2014

Contents

Introduction

Many people can take a good photo — in fact, many people can take a great photo. But this book is about something else. This book is about how to be a photographer.

I want to challenge you with two questions:

o If you take a photo and no one sees it, what was the point?
o If you take a photo that's ignored by everyone who sees it, what was the point?

To be a photographer, you have to understand more than just the image — you have to understand the interaction between the image and the viewer, and you have to choose what you want that interaction to be. There should be an intent behind taking a photo and showing it to people. Your job as the photographer is to answer the question, "What impact do I want my photo to have on its viewer?"

Deciding on the intent is what it means to be a photographer. It's not about taking a correctly exposed, well-focused photo, nor is it about the ability to take slow-exposure water shots. It's not about using HDR to expand the dynamic range, using multiple lighting setups like a pro, capturing the perfect portrait, or finding the one decisive moment that truly captures a scene. These technical and artistic skills are important, but if they're all you have, you're not a photographer.

Being a photographer also has nothing to do with making money; that's a business skill. Many photographers never make any money from photography, because it's not important to being a photographer. Just browse through sites like Flickr, 500px, and Instagram, and you'll find some fantastic hobbyist photographers who never even try to make money. On the other hand, it's possible (though harder) to make money from simply taking photos without caring about the impact they'll have. For example, taking stock photos, while incredibly difficult and only for the skilled, is something I think of as different from photography.

I'm not trying to say that technical, artistic, and business skills are unimportant, or that you shouldn't study them. You should. Read about these skills, go to workshops, and practice them constantly. These skills are essential and you won't get far in photography without them, but they're not enough to make you a photographer. To be a photographer, you need to understand intent.

If you agree with me that a photo that never gets looked at is a waste, ask yourself, "Why would someone look at my photos?" My argument is that you, as a photographer, have to have an intent. The intent is the impact you want your photo to have on someone when they look at it. This means not only being aware of intent as a concept, but actively choosing this intent before taking your photo.

My approach to this is to figure out and understand who's going to be looking at my photos from the very beginning. Who's my audience? What do they want when they're looking at my photos, and what am I going to give them?

In the following chapters, I cover a series of projects, each based on a different audience. I'll start with the most important person looking at your pictures, the only person who will look at every photo you take: you! Then I'll gradually expand the projects to include more and more people. For each project, I invite you to think about the desired outcome, what photos you need to take, how to go about getting the photos, and finally, what to do with the photos once you have them.

I won't be talking about ISO, shutter speed, aperture and the like because this is not a book about technique. However as you go though the projects don't forget to work on your technical skill. Technical knowledge of how to take a good photo is something that comes with practice. The time you spend taking photos for these projects is valuable behind the camera experience and you should make the most of the opportunity to develop your technical skills.

This is a short book. My intent is that it will take you at most a few hours to read from cover to cover, though if you follow through and actually do all the projects, it could easily take a year. I hope that, by the end of this process, thinking about the intent behind your photos has become a natural and automatic part of your photography.

For Yourself

You can have many different intents when taking a photo. You get to choose which intent you want, but you have to decide who will see your photos before you can choose what reaction you want them to have.

I want to start you off thinking about intent by considering what reaction you want yourself to have when you look at your own photos. You get to choose what you think your reaction should be, but I recommend the intent of liking your own photos. You will see every photo you take — and you're probably the only person who will. If you don't like your own photos, you'll find that's not much fun.

It's easy to figure out what types of photos you like. Start by looking at photos other people have taken and making a list. The internet has thousands of photos you can browse though, and your local bookshop will have a photography section where you can find books by famous photographers. Start flipping through the pages, and if you find yourself looking at a photo for more than a few seconds, ask yourself what stands out about it. There are no right (or wrong) answers — it could be the colours, the sky, the expressions of people in the photos, or even a sense of curiosity about what happened next. There are absolutely no rules; anything that captures your attention is good enough to go on your list.

Go through your own photos, as well. Spend just a few seconds on each one, and see which ones make you pause. When you find yourself looking at the same photo for more than a few seconds, ask yourself the same question: "What stood out?"

Include what you like when looking at both your own and others' photos on your list. When you write something down, your brain pays more attention to it — plus you can come back and look at it again in the future if you're forgetful (like me). It doesn't matter if the list seems too big or too small. All that matters is that there are some things you like about some photos.

When I went through this exercise with my own photos, I discovered I'm attracted to ones that:

- are technically interesting — the kind that make me stop and wonder how I got that look. What was the shutter speed? How was the lighting done?
- capture my personal interpretation of a moment. These are the photos I can show other people and say, "This is what I see."

When I like one of my photos, it always meets one of these two parameters; however, it doesn't work the other way. Sometimes there's a photo that meets one or even both of these criteria, yet when I look at it, it leaves me feeling flat. There's clearly a third element my own photos must have before I like them: They have to appeal to my own personal aesthetic taste.

Very few photographers know what they'd put on their personal list when they first pick up a camera. But as they practice and reflect on their photos, they gradually start to understand which photos appeal to them and which don't. This is the beginning of developing a personal style.

If you want to develop your own personal style, you need to focus on taking photos for yourself — photos that you want to look at, that aren't taken for anyone other than you. Remember that professional photographers are often paid to take photos they would never have chosen to take, or in a style they don't prefer. If you're being paid to take photos, it's important to invest time in exploring your own personal style.

When it comes to exploring your personal style further, remember the best way to learn more about something is with firsthand experience. Start actively getting experience in working with whatever ended up on your list. Planning a small shoot or project around one or a few of these ideas is a great way to understand more about what captured your attention in the first place, as well as a chance to learn the technique needed to recreate it. If for example, you find yourself fascinated with photos that use multiple off-camera lights to convey emotions and mood then plan some personal shoots based on these skills. As you do the shoots you will be learning both the techniques and how you feel about different effects.

As you do this, remember that you'll be your own harshest critic. There will always be lots of things you can't stand about your own photos. No matter how much time you spend changing where you stand, how you ask your subjects to behave, etc., the photos just won't be what you wanted — and the few you do like were accidents.

This happens to every single photographer on the planet, but that doesn't make it any easier to deal with. Just remember that everyone is in the same boat, and that for every great photo you see, hundreds or maybe thousands of terrible photos were thrown away. Don't lose heart; keep looking for the things you like in your photos, and you'll start to find that some stand out. These are the photos you like — the photos you've taken for yourself.

There's one obvious question now: What do you do with the photos you've taken for yourself?

There is one really wrong answer: Put them on a hard disk and never look at them (uploading them to Facebook or Flickr and never looking at them is the same thing). The important thing is that once you have taken photos for yourself, you should look at and appreciate them.

Traditionally, you do this by building a portfolio: a collection of your best photos. Creating a physical portfolio with proper binding and so on can be very expensive, not to mention a real pain when you want to add a photo to it, but digital-portfolio apps for tablets and phones are now available.

You can also have your photos printed and framed, and hang your favourites up at home. If you're worried about your friends thinking you have a big head, print small sizes, so they're not obvious.

My personal favourite is to set the home screen of your computer or phone to show a selection of your best photos. That way, they get put in front of you rather than sitting away somewhere you might never see them. After all, what's the point of taking photos you love if you're never going to look at them?

For Your Family

Now that I've covered taking photos for yourself, I'll discuss taking photos for other people. This is an important subject, because there are lots of different people out there. To keep things easy, I'm going to categorise them into several easy-to-understand groups, starting with a group of people you probably know very well: your family.

Your family members are the easiest people to take photos for — you spend a lot of time with them, and for better or worse, they helped you become who you are. Their values and opinions probably influenced your own, and you know them well enough to know what's important to them and what interests and inspires them. You know what types of art they like and what values they have. In short, you know exactly what they'd like to see in photos.

Remember, though, that unless your family members are photographers themselves, what they consider a good picture is going to be very different from you. Chances are they don't care about focus, for example, whereas whenever you look at a photo, your photographer's eye probably starts to look at it immediately: Is it sharp? Is the depth of field right? Is it in the right place, such as the eyes?

It took me a long time to learn one simple lesson: No one else cares! Normal people (i.e., those unaffected by the burning desire to buy a new lens) are far more concerned about whether their smiles look good, whether their arms look fat, and what they're wearing. I've lost track of the number of times I've felt disappointed when someone has grabbed one of my photos, told me how wonderful it is, and then told me it's of her wearing her favourite dress when I asked what she liked about it.

Don't get me wrong—it's still crucial to have a well-composed, well-exposed, and well-focused photo. But as soon as you start taking photos for other people to enjoy, those details have to take a backseat to whatever the viewer wants to see.

This is why family members are so easy to take photos for: You already know what they want to see. I know my grandmother always wants to see photos of her grandchildren, so if I want to take a photo for her, I don't have to struggle to find a suitable subject. For my dad, I know it's old furniture — especially chairs and derelict buildings. My mother likes photos that tell the sort of story in which you wonder what the person in the photo is doing or about to do next.
Most families also have their own history, jokes, and traditions, which can be very important. For example, as a

child, I used to love Christmas Eve even more than Christmas Day. I was always allowed to open one present early, which felt like beating the system. These types of moments are perfect subject matter for photos, and who else but you will capture them for your family?

Knowing what to take photos of isn't the only reason it's easy to take photos for your family. This might sound like a bit of a cheat (and it totally is), but the fact is that your family members are probably going to like a photo purely because you took it. Family can be sentimental like that.

Sentiment is important because photos evoke memories, and most people value memories of their family. Imagine your sister has just given birth to her first child. Do you think she'd value a baby portrait taken by a stranger more than one taken by you? Even if the stranger's photo is better, it only evokes the memory of one family member, while the photo you took is associated with memories of two.

Taking photos of your family is also really easy since they're always around, and therefore readily available for candid photos. Simply having your camera with you whenever you spend time with your family will give you more opportunities than you can imagine. A lot of good family photos are candid with no formal setup needed, but when you want to get a bit more creative, those close to you are normally easiest to persuade to sit while you rig up some lights.

When I got my first set of studio lights, I built a studio in our spare room. It really wasn't great — a black cloth from a local curtain store provided the background, and to this day my mum reminds me how I tried to get her to iron the creases out of the whole thing (it was about three meters wide and five meters long!). It was held up on some half-inch-thick copper plumbers' pipe we asked our plumber to weld together on one visit. The power cables for the lights were a serious health hazard — and that's not to mention the risk of being hit by falling copper pipes. Yet I still managed to persuade my entire family to come through one (sometimes two) at a time and have their portraits taken. By the time I finished that day, I had a photo of my grandfather and uncle that we ended up doing a copy of for everyone in the family.

A nice bonus of taking photos for your family is that it solves the question of what to give them for birthday and Christmas presents. Giving someone a framed print of a photo taken especially for them can be a very touching gesture. It's common for someone to appreciate a photo taken for them by a family member so much that they want to display it to guests. So typically, when I'm taking photos like this, I'll give a print rather than a digital copy.

For Close Friends

Throughout this book, I'm going to try and persuade you to look at who you take photos for and stretch yourself to take the next step. This continuous stretching will force you to grow as a photographer; without it, you'll find yourself getting stuck taking the same photos again and again. So while taking photos of your family is hugely rewarding both for you and them, it's time to try something just a bit harder: your friends.

Friends are, by definition, friendly. Automatically, that brings a whole bag full of advantages. It's easy to access them, and they'll put up with you shoving a camera in their face (at least for a while). And they care enough about you to give your photos at least a quick look, if not more. But don't be fooled into thinking photographing your friends is as easy as it sounds.

It's not uncommon for people to say they feel a closer connection to their friends than their family — after all, you chose your friends, but not your family. Personally, I think it's because you probably don't know your friends as well as you know your family. You usually haven't known them for as long, and they may be hiding many of their problems from you. That can be a good thing in a friendship, but means there may be aspects of your friends you don't know about — unlike your family, whom you've lived with your whole life and seen at their best and worst. Be warned: That can lead to some issues (and not just when taking photos).

I love taking photos of my friends. Whenever I get a new lens, light modifier, or gadget of one form or another, I want to try it out, and it's my friends who get picked on and end up being in these pictures. If I have new bit of kit and it's portable, then I'll take it with me when I hang out with friends and play around with it. These photos sometimes end up with a startled-looking friend standing in the middle of a park or bar. These photos get deleted - even when a photo is technically okay, I never see the point of keeping a photo showing my friends looking like shocked lemons.

My friends don't want to see shocked-lemon photos either. What they want to see is something that reminds them of the fun we have hanging out together. That's the best intent I've found when I want my friends to see my photos — I want them to be reminded of the common bonds that form our friendship. I want them to look at the photos and say things like, "Oh, I remember that! Do you remember what happened just after you took this? That was when…"

One option is to ask your friends to do a portrait session with you. Set aside some time and find somewhere nice, like a park or even a plain brick wall, and spend an hour taking photos of them. This can feel a bit forced, making your friends feel too much on the spot, and for this reason can be a great way to practice putting people at ease. However, if you don't get photos that remind you of the fun you had with your friends, then just stick to taking photos while hanging out with them.

When I hang out with my friends, if I take the camera (it's nice not to sometimes — in fact, most of the time), I'm thinking about capturing a memory of the evening: Who was there? How did they behave? What happened to them? I really love this type of photography because of its mix of portraiture and documentary. Each of my friends has something unique about their personality — something that makes them special — and if a photo doesn't show that, it's missing an important part of the memory.

I have to struggle to get this right while also dealing with the technical situation (bad lighting, cramped space, etc.) that I often have no control over. And as if that's not enough, there's the challenge of capturing that evening in particular rather than a random period of time. It's not enough to just have a series of portraits and no idea of where we were. For example, if we go to a bar, each bar has a unique feel to it that's part of the evening. If we're out hiking, the weather is such a huge part of the day that it deserves some photos too. I also try to capture what happened to friends on that day. Did someone get upset, or spill a drink all over themselves? Everything that happens while hanging out with friends is part of a memory.

It's not just your time together that you can show your friends photos of. I bet there's much more to each of your friends than just being someone to hang out with. They're people, and people have passions — hobbies they obsess about. They could be anything: sports, gardening, their pets, military re-enactments, or any one of literally millions of things. The more they obsess about something, the more they'll care about good photos of it. One of the most surefire ways to know someone will want to see your work is to take photos of something they obsess about. Ask yourself what passions your friends have, and how can you start taking photos of those passions.

After you've taken the photos, your friends are going to want to see them. They'll also want to keep them so they can look at them in the future, and probably want to show them to other people. This is what Facebook was made for; these are exactly the sort of photos to upload to a Facebook album. You friends will start to engage with them, leaving comments and so on, and your reputation as someone who takes good photos reliably will start to grow beyond your family.

Another thing I love to do for my friends is print a photo book of any time we spend together that's especially significant. Holidays are perfect for this. I typically take a few thousand photos on a holiday and narrow them down to about 100 photos. It's so easy now to get a photo book printed. You can put the book together and send your friends a link, so they can buy a copy if they want to. Personally, I buy a copy for myself and make sure anyone else can buy a copy at cost. I'm not looking to make a profit from my friends!

To Help Your Friends

So far, I've discussed taking photos for yourself, your family, and your friends: people you know. But these photos will be seen by some people you don't know, as well — your grandmother will show your photos to her friends, the photos of your holiday with your friends will be seen by their friends, etc. But this is incidental, or maybe even accidental; the intent was for the photos to be seen by people you know. Now, for the first time, I'm going to encourage you to take photos with the hope that people you don't know will look at them.

This is a big change. It's hard enough to put yourself in the mind of someone you know and ask how they'd react, but it's much easier than doing the same thing with a stranger.

To keep this manageable and not too scary, try tying it in with helping your friends and family achieve their goals. Start asking them what they're trying to do. Is your best friend a budding comedian trying to get his first gig? Is your sister a jeweller trying to sell her jewellery? Does your cousin own a blog with a message he's trying to spread? Is your college roommate a performer, trying to get her name out there? Is your uncle a runner, trying to raise money by running a marathon? I've found that nearly everyone I ask has a story they're trying to tell. If you start to ask around, I'm sure some of your friends and family will have projects they're working on. Your photos can help these projects.

When I started taking photos to help friends and family, I found the hardest part was working out how photos can help them. It's a new skill — beyond the normal technical or artistic skills a photographer needs. Nothing you know about shutter speeds, ISO settings, or what makes a good composition will help you. It's a case-by-case situation, but there are a few ways of thinking about it that might help.

You can create a visual image. One friend of mine is a burlesque performer, trying to gain recognition on the London burlesque circuit. She can use photos to build her website, Facebook page, and personal brand about her burlesque alter ego. We worked for several afternoons to produce some photos, which she used to present her image to her growing fan base. I took the photos for her, but my intent was that her fans would be the ones looking at them — fans that I, as the photographer, don't know.

You can tell a story. Another friend of mine ran the London Marathon recently. To get a spot in the race, she had to raise a certain amount of money through sponsorship. She started by contacting friends through e-mail and social networks, asking them to sponsor her, and some did. To make this work better, we took some photos of her running and training. These photos become artifacts that told her story: the story of working hard, of the time and commitment she'd been putting into training, and of how much time and effort has gone into raising money. She then shared the photos with friends who, in turn, shared them with their friends — none of whom I even know the name of.

You can give a fact clarity. Haje recently started a company, TriggerTrap, that produces an iPhone and Android app allowing photographers to trigger the shutter in their camera to respond to sound, light, and a number of other things. The first version (the v1) was not an app, but a physical device, and was intentionally quite hacky — that is to say, it had exposed circuit boards and didn't have a fancy case. It was important that customers ordering a TriggerTrap v1 over the Web understood what to expect, because if they were expecting something with the design quality of an iPhone, they'd be upset. So the website Haje built was full of photos of the device and circuit boards, which are a bright orange-red and strangely picturesque. There's no way any shoppers looking over the website can fail to get a clear understanding of what they're ordering.

Once you've worked out how you want the photos to help your friends and family, it's time to take them. How you do this is really going to depend on what photos you want to take. Almost certainly, you'll need to book some of your time and some of your friends' and family's time. This is an important experience for you, and your friends and family members will have to take on the role of customer. They understand the people you're intending to influence and you (probably) don't, and so they will have valid opinions on what photos you need to create.

This is the first time I've suggested adding someone else's opinion into the creative process of what is, at the end of the day, your photography. Back at the beginning of this book, I spoke about it being important to personally like the photos you take. That is still true, and I think it should always be true. It's just that if your friends are going to use the photos, then their intent, and their opinions on how to achieve that intent have to be taken into consideration.

My approach to this is that after the shoot, I go back to my computer, sort and rate my photos, and produce a shortlist of those I'm happy with, which I send to the friend or family member I photographed. For practical reasons, I typically send small JPEG files. The recipient gets to reject any he doesn't like, and tell me which ones he does like. That way, we end up with a collection of photos we both agree are good and worth using. Then I send him either high-res JPEG or TIFF files if he's planning on using the photos for high-quality printing.

When you're taking photos with the intent that a friend or family member will use them, often the best way to present them is with a collection of digital files. This is the only time I don't see any point in thinking about photo presentation — that becomes the job of your friend or family member.

To Help Strangers

In the previous chapter, I encouraged you to start taking photos that would be seen by people beyond your immediate group of friends and family. Once you've done so, it's a good idea to try working with and taking photos of people you don't know so well. I've called this chapter "To Help Strangers", but I want to narrow that down just a little bit; there are so many strangers in the world, and we need to start somewhere.

Most of us spend time with a group of people who share a common interest. The interest could be a hobby, job, social group, or something else altogether. As long as there are a reasonable number of people in the group and not all of them are close friends, it will serve the purpose I have in mind.

What I suggest is trying to document day-to-day events that make up life in this group. Build a living record of the people and events, and try to show how it feels to be part of the group. This will push you to learn two important new skills.

First, you'll have to learn how to work with people who might not welcome having a camera shoved in their faces. You'll have to win them over, and persuade them to give you a chance.

Secondly, you'll need to learn to find the feeling of a group, and how to capture it in a photo or series of photos. Once you can do this, you have to prove it to everyone else — that you can turn your photos into something that becomes an important part of the memories in the group for years to come. For some people, this will be scary, so the best thing to do is jump in at the deep end.

You should have some direction for the photos you're taking, and let people know in advance that you're going to be about with your camera. It gives people a chance to do their hair, or let you know if they don't want their photos taken.

Start by trying what I've done several times: Set up a portrait session. Tell everyone in the group you'd like to give them a set of good photos of everyone. Bring some lights or find a spot with good daylight, sit everyone down, and take a portrait or two.

I also like to ask if anyone objects to me trying to get some candid portraits while the group is doing something else, as well. These candids are your chance to try and capture the feel of the group.

First, you need to have the freedom to take photos. Not only do you need to get permission, but it's important for everyone to be comfortable enough with you and your camera for you to take photos while normal life continues uninterrupted. The best way to do that is to start taking photos without getting in the way. These early photos probably won't be good, but they'll help people relax. In the pre-digital days, I heard of photographers who'd shoot without film in their camera for just this reason.

Once you've done that, you can concentrate on learning what photos really grab the feel of the day-to-day environment. I have two techniques I rely on for this.

One is to ask yourself what feelings you experience when you're in this group of people. Keep that in mind while you look about and observe them going about what they're doing. See what specific things remind you of the feeling you want to capture, and then see if you can get it in a photo.

The alternative is to concentrate on the biggest personalities: the people who set the tone for everything else. Get good photos of them, and you have 90 percent of the group's dynamic recorded. Then you just need to fill in photos of the rest of the people. Don't fall into the trap of thinking that will be easy, though — each person will present their own set of problems when you try to get good photos of them.

Once you start taking these photos, you'll begin to be known as the person with a camera, and people will start accepting having you and the camera about. It's really important that people begin to trust you, so make sure people only see your better shots. Don't let too many people see the shots that didn't work out or look bad; that's not a reputation you want to have.

By this point, you'll have built up enough trust that everyone is happy for you and your camera to come to events. I think events are the best part of any group of people. For many years, I've been a member of a Latin and Ballroom Dancing club, and I love taking my camera to competitions. There is so much happening; I regularly get photos of dancers getting ready, waiting by the edge of the floor to compete, celebrating a win, or experiencing the pain of a bad result, as well as of the audience enjoying a particular performance. This is the really great thing about events: There's so much happening that you'll have no trouble finding something wonderful to take photos of.

If you do all this, you'll soon build an awesome body of work and will then just need to figure out the best way to present it. I'm a huge fan of photo books for this. You can do one for each calendar year, or even for each event if the events are big. If you keep taking group photos and putting them in books, you'll quickly build up a library that will become a key part of the group's living history. This is exactly what taking photos of a group of people is all about.

Another option is to turn your photos into an online archive. To be honest, I'm not a huge fan of this, because I've never seen it done well. Typically, the photos end up getting lost or even deleted in a website redesign or similar situation. If you find a good way of making this work, let me know!

For Your Passion

If you've been following along and doing the projects in previous chapters, you should now have a solid skillset. Even though I've not explicitly addressed them, your technical, artistic, and people skills will have had a lot of practice, and you should be comfortable with them. Now that those skills are sorted, it's time to really put them to use and make a wider impact in the world. Take photos of something you're passionate about — something you dream about every day — to share that passion with the world. The intent of this chapter is to make other people feel the same passion you do.

The first step is to work out what your passion is. It could be a hobby, a good cause, or a philosophy. It could be as general as travel, as specific as surfing on west-coast beaches in the southern hemisphere. Or it can be somewhere in between, like surfing or beaches.

My personal passion is dancing. While at university, I spent a long time as a member of the university dance club. Eventually I realised competitive dancing appealed to more than any other form of dancing, or even the social group surrounding the university dance team. More specifically, while the team had two disciplines — Ballroom and Latin American — I realised quickly that I found Latin American dancing far more interesting, energetic, and photogenic than Ballroom.

Before you go out and start taking photos to share with the world, take a few minutes to think about who your possible audiences are and your specific intentions. Broadly speaking, the audience can be categorised into three groups: people who share your passion, people who know about the subject without being passionate about it, and people who know nothing about the subject. Each group will react very differently to the same set of photos, so spend some time deciding which group you want to target. There's an old saying, "You can't please all of the people all of the time," that really applies here, which is why it's important to pick a target group that works with your intentions for sharing your passion. Do you want to become a known expert within the subject? Do you want to teach your friends about your passion? Or do you want to inspire many more people to become passionate about your subject?

If it's the first answer, your target group will be people already passionate about the subject. If it's the second, you should target people who already know about your passion. And if it's the last answer, you're targeting everyone in the world! Personally, I think the third answer — inspiring many, many more people to become passionate about your subject — is the most interesting.

Your choice of target group and intention is going to have some implications when it comes to finding people to show your photos to. If you want to become a known expert in the subject and know a lot of people who share your passion, that group will be easy to find. If you're trying to explain to your friends why you're passionate about your subject, you already know your target group. On the other hand, if you want to change the general public perception of your passion, you'll know very few of the people you're trying to reach.

Now that you have a clear idea of what you're aiming to do, it's time to get started. The approach we're going to take is to break down the elements of your passion, focus on which elements you can capture in photographs, and then work out which of those shots will achieve your goal.

First comes deconstructing the subject. I should point out that not everyone agrees with this approach. Many people feel that if you break something with a magical and mystical feel down into its parts, you'll lose the magic. I think they're wrong — I've always found the exact opposite. The more I break down a subject, the more detail I go into, and the more magic I find.

Grab a piece of paper, and start to write down the main ideas you'd talk about if you were going to explain your passion to your grandmother. If I did this about dancing, my list would look something like this:

o The energy

- The shapes (that the dancers make with their bodies)
- The preparation
- The interplay between man and woman
- The music
- The costumes

Some of these will be easy to take photos of (just writing the list brings images to my mind), while others are more conceptual and thus a lot harder.

Move any item that will be hard to take a photo of to the bottom of your list. For the items that are easy or possible to photograph, work out which will have the biggest contribution to your intent. If you want to establish yourself as an expert, then which ones let you demonstrate your knowledge of the subject best? If you're explaining your passion, which one most capture the magical feeling you have? Once you've worked out which ones will best suit your intent, move them to the top of your list.

Starting at the top of your list and working your way down, write out some ideas for what the photos would look like. Where would they need to be taken? Who (if anyone) is in them? How should you light them? What you're doing now is preparing a shot list of the photos you're going to take.

Go through the list again, but this time, think about the practicalities of how you could take each photo. What's the right equipment to use? Do you need special access to people or locations? Do you need anyone to help you?

Then go through again, this time moving the easiest shots (based on your notes) to the top of the list. The idea is to ensure the first shots you take come out well. This is a great trick for maintaining motivation on a big project. Once you see that you've had some initial success, it's easier to go for the harder, more complex shots; you'll know that if they don't work, it doesn't matter because you already have some shots in the bag.

Now go through your list one last time — but this time, go out and take the pictures.

Be warned: This will take a while — possibly several months. But by the end of the list, you'll have a collection of hopefully great photos. Unfortunately, that isn't good enough; you can't stop yet. If you go around showing people great photos, they'll certainly marvel at your skill and tell you how wonderful you are, but that's not what you're trying to accomplish here!

You need to test your photos to see if they get the reaction from other people that you wanted them to get. Prepare your photos to show your friends by printing them or putting them on your phone or tablet. For the moment, the format doesn't matter — what matters is that you can sit down next to a friend and bring out the photos. Sit down with your friends one at a time, show them the photos, and ask what feelings the photos provoke in them.

It's really important to ask about feelings here, because otherwise you'll get comments about the focus, colours, and composition. These sorts of comments are great for improving your technical skills, but won't tell you if the photos are achieving your intent. When I do this with dance photos, what I'm looking for more than anything is for my friend to say, "Wow, now I really want to come and watch a competition." Showing the photos to friends and asking about feelings is a useful technique even when your eventual target group is not your friends. If your friends react well to your photos, chances are your target group will as well.

After you've sat with your friends and talked about the photos, you'll be able to narrow them down to the ones that generated the right reaction. These are the photos you need to start sharing.

When working out how to show these photos you have to remember that they are a set, and really need to be shown as a set. This gives you several options to choose between.

Facebook lets you group photos into an album and move forward and backwards between them, which is good. However Facebook is really targeted at people you know, and maybe their friends. This can either be really good or really bad, depending on which audience you chose to take the photos for. If you chose an audience you are well connected with on Facebook then this is great. However if you chose an audience mostly consisting of strangers then it's a problem.

A second option is to build a dedicated website for your project. If you have the computer skills to do this then it can be a cheap and easy option. Unfortunately if you don't know how to do it and have to rely on someone else then custom building a site will probably be too expensive, but there are many blogging platforms or portfolio sites that can do the job. Taking this approach has almost the exact opposite issues to Facebook. It's a lot harder to get people to look at your project, but everyone can look at it.

You also have the option of doing something in the physical world. I've mentioned creating a book several times already, and that's an option. Alternatively you could think about an exhibition. It's harder to set up: either you have to get someone to pay for the exhibition space and printing costs or you have to do it yourself. However it can work really well, especially if you are targeting a group of people who hold a regular meeting or a festival or something similar. In that case many of the people you want to target will be in the same physical location, so it makes sense to make the photos big, visible, and somewhere where they can't miss them.

Hopefully, if you've been following the previous projects in this book, you'll have already amassed a number of fans who like your photography for various reasons. The next step is to contact them and let them know your project is ready.

For Clients

As you learn to be a photographer, start taking better and better photos, and get your photos seen by more and more people, it's almost inevitable that at some point someone will ask how much you'd charge to take photos for them. Welcome to the world of working with clients.

Working with clients isn't an essential step to becoming a great photographer; in fact, many photographers have made the decision not to work for someone else, and to only do work they really want to do. This is because there are many downsides to working for someone else. However, there are a lot of positives: Working with a client can force you to develop in ways you otherwise wouldn't. Plus, you can get paid for it, which isn't bad either. So if you get the chance, I say go for it.

Let's start off by looking at the negative sides of working for a client, since forewarned is forearmed. Broadly speaking, the problems are loss of control, risk of failing, and lack of experimental freedom.

Your client probably has a very good idea of what she wants the photo to look like; it's not uncommon for her to already be able to visualise the end photo in her mind. She wants you to recreate that image. At this point, she reduces your photography to a technical and logistical exercise: Can you find a location that fits her image? Can you find the right models (if needed)? Do you know how to set up that lighting technique? I've spent the last few chapters arguing that being a photographer is about a lot more than the technical elements. Challenging and skillful as this work is, it isn't what I mean when I talk about being a photographer. You have little to no control over the images themselves, which can pose a problem.

Next is the risk that you will fail and come back without a single workable image. This is really scary to think about when you consider that someone else is placing trust in you to do a good job, and is paying you for your time. I always feel a sense of responsibility to produce a decent image. This can make you nervous, which will in turn make it harder to do a good job.

To overcome this nervousness, it's best to use techniques you know well. Stick with a simple one-light setup you understand, poses for the model you've worked with a hundred times before, or whatever most makes sense, given the subject. This means you'll know you can get a decent, workable shot, but it can become boring and repetitive both for you personally and your photos, which will also start to become boring and repetitive.

The last of the three problems when working with clients is the lack of freedom to experiment. When doing work you've initiated yourself, you can play with whatever ideas you want to, and if nothing good comes of it, it's okay. Since you're free from the constraint of having a useable shot in the bag at the end of the day, you can push yourself to work with new lighting setups or new locations, develop new technical skills, and grow your knowledge. This may not be the case with client work.

On the other hand, there are some real opportunities to push yourself to improve when you work with a client — the most obvious being that you have to really hone and sharpen your existing technical skills. You can't fail, so you have to be able to get a workable shot — no matter what! This means you need to spend time getting to know your camera, lenses, and lights, and know what you can expect from them.

However, I'm much more interested in the other way you can push yourself with client work. Remember: My general principles for being a photographer are to focus on who will see the photos and the point of the photos. In an ideal world, the client would be able to simply tell you the answer to both of these questions; in the real world, she probably can't, so you're going to have to work out the answers. The skill you need to learn here is how to see through whatever brief the client has given you, and work out what she's trying to accomplish. What does she want the photos to do? Once you know her goal, start to think about how she'll get people to look at the photos. I've covered this a bit in the previous chapters, so by now you should have an idea of some of the normal options: books, websites, prints, etc. Once you understand this, you can get to work on taking the photos.

While you're doing all this thinking about what photos to take, whatever you do, don't forget the original brief! Hopefully you've managed to understand the intent behind the brief and worked out what sort of photos will really do what the client wants, but the brief is still the brief.

Imagine the client is a jewellery maker, and has asked you for pictures of a pretty girl wearing red. You've worked out what he really wants is for you to create an image that associates his jewellery with a classy evening out. You might decide the best way to capture that intent is a series of photos at a high-end cocktail bar, of people queuing to get into the opera, or of someone in an expensive dress, running in the rain trying to get to shelter — all wearing nice jewellery, of course. But no matter what sort of photos you choose, they'd better include a pretty girl wearing red!

The real trick to working with a client is to realise there are two different audiences and goals to consider, as well as the now-familiar idea of thinking about who will be looking at the final photos and why, there is an initial audience, and that's the client. The first person who will see your photos is not the end viewer — it's the client.

You want your photo to do two things when the client looks at it. First, he has to see that you've followed his brief/instructions. Secondly, he has to believe his audience members will have the right reaction when they see the photos. This may be a completely different question from whether you, as the photographer, believe the audience will have the right reaction to the photos.

If the client thinks you've met the brief but doesn't think the images will do what he wants, you'll get paid, but the client probably won't publish the photos. Your work will never get seen, and you probably won't get hired by that client again. It doesn't matter if the photos really would've had the desired effect; if the client doesn't think so, he probably won't publish them.

If the client thinks the photos won't have the desired effect and you didn't meet the brief, not only will he not publish the photos, but there's a chance he'll try to not pay you. Not good.

It's possible to succeed if you ignore the brief; if you still get photos the client thinks will have the desired effect, he may decide the actual brief wasn't that important. But that's difficult, and a big risk. If you want to try this, don't say I didn't warn you!

Once you have photos the client likes and thinks will have the right effect, your job is almost done. Typically, you'll give the client digital copies of the files, and he worries about how to get the images in front of the audience. So that, at least, is one question taken off your mind.

For Yourself

The real message I had in mind when I sat down to write this book takes the form of a question: Why do you want to be a photographer, and what do you want to achieve? By this, I mean something beyond the impact created by a single photo, a single shoot, or a photo project.

Throughout the previous chapters, I've used individual projects to introduce the idea that photography has an impact, and by keeping the impact you want to make in mind while working on a shoot, you can move from being a GWC (Guy With Camera or Girl With Camera) to being a photographer. If you get into the habit of regularly focusing on the impact you intend to make for each project you work on, sooner or later you're going to start to make an impact. As you complete more and more projects, the impact starts to add up, and then there's a deeper question: What specific impact are you trying to make with the combination of all the photos you take?

This is your choice. There is no right or wrong answer — it's a question each photographer has to work out for themselves — but I can offer you some help on how to think about it.

First of all, one thing is guaranteed: Being a photographer is going to have a direct impact on your life. So the first important question you need to answer is: What impact do you want photography to have on your life?

To help you work this out, consider the following questions:

- o Do you want a hobby to help you relax at the weekends?
- o Do you want to explore and learn about art?
- o Do you want to make a living?

I don't intend for this to include everything photography can do for you; I'm simply hoping to get you thinking toward working out the right answer for you.

After you've chosen what impact you want photography to have on your life, you can also consider what impact you want to create beyond that, if any. You could argue that as long as some people are looking at your photos, having an impact beyond yourself is unavoidable. The real question, though, is whether you want to have a driving focus behind all of your photography. For example, look at photographers like Don McCullin, who has shown the world what the reality of war looks like, or Mario Testino, who has helped create a worldwide shared view of high fashion. Again, there's no right or wrong answer to this question — it's a choice each photographer has to make individually.

If you decide you do want a consistent, driving intent behind all your work, your options are limitless. There are so many things you can choose that I'm not going to even attempt to list them. That, as my university lecturers would've told me, is an "exercise left to the reader."

Summary

So that's it. All you have to do to become a photographer is practice using intent. Throughout this book I've suggested several projects that you should do. The idea is that you work though them and get first hand experience. Experience that will develop your understanding of intent more than reading one book ever can.

Below is a recap of the projects I've suggested, for easy reference.

For yourself.
Intent: Work out what you like.
Project: Look though all the photos you admire and all the photos you have taken so far. Create a list of what appeals to you about the photos you like. Plan a shoot to practice using those things in your photography. Take the keepers from this shoot and put them somewhere you will see them. On your computer desktop or smartphone home screen, for example.

For your family.

Intent: Take photos your family will love
Project: Arrange some shoots with your family members. Use your knowledge of them to design shots that will be valued and treasured by specific members of your family. Turn the photos into framed prints and give to them as gifts.

For close friends.
Intent: Remind your friends (and yourself) of the fun you have together.
Project: Take photos of the time you spend with your friends. Whether it's going out to bars, hanging out in the park or going on holiday together. Whatever it is you do with your friends when you all get together. Post the photos into a Facebook album, maybe even create a book.

To help your friends
Intent: Help your friends reach their goals
Project: Talk to your friends and work out what it is they are trying to achieve. Figure out a way that photos can help them achieve their goals. Once you've done that, plan and shoot the necessary photos. Pass the photos onto your friend who can then use them (make sure they know how you think the photo can help).

To help strangers
Intent: Build a living record of a group
Project: Choose a group of people that you are part of or can easily spend time with. It could be your work place, a group of people who share a hobby or a local community movement. Learn how to fit in with the group so that you can take photos

comfortably and without disrupting their normal behaviours with your camera. Take portraits of the key personalities, cover the main events, and then fill in the gaps. Turn your photos into a book and present it to people in the group.

For your passion
Intent: Inspire people with your passion
Project: Identify what you are passionate about. Then decide exactly who you want to inspire and what part of your passion you think is going to be inspirational to them. Take the photos that you think will convey the passion and then display them. If you're trying to reach friends of friends then Facebook is a great way to show them. If you are not trying to reach friends of friends then build a website as a digital exhibition space, or create a real physical exhibition.

For clients
Intent: Whatever the client wants to do
Project: Work out what your client wants to do, and if the photos they have asked you for will achieve that. If not work out what photos will. Plan a shoot and get photos that will do both what the client wants, and meet the brief the client gave you. You might have to do these as two different sets of photos if you think the client's brief won't achieve their intent. Give the photos to the client in whatever format they want them.

For yourself
Intent: Work out why you are taking photos
Project: Have a long think about your deeper intent. Not just why you are doing a given shoot, but what you want to achieve

with photography in general. There are no wrong answers to this question, except maybe "I don't know".

Afterword

Thank you for taking the time to read my book. Remember these are my opinions, which you may or may not agree with, and that's OK. Either way I welcome feedback. I can be found online at www.wildfalcon.com and you can contact me by sending me an email on laurie@wildfalcon.com or via twitter, where I can be found as @LRY_Photo. I can't always respond but I read every message.

If you liked this book, or if it made you think, the best form of praise is a recommendation. I'd love it if you would recommend this book to at least two of your friends.